Under Memories of Stars

poems by

Natalie Marino

Finishing Line Press
Georgetown, Kentucky

Under Memories of Stars

For my family

Copyright © 2023 by Natalie Marino
ISBN 979-8-88838-254-7 First Edition
All rights reserved under International and Pan-American Copyright Conventions. No part of this book may be reproduced in any manner whatsoever without written permission from the publisher, except in the case of brief quotations embodied in critical articles and reviews.

ACKNOWLEDGMENTS

Thank you to the journal editors who first published these poems, some in different forms:

The Aurora Journal: "April Rain," "Jouissance"
Bitter Oleander: "Constellation of Seeds"
Capsule Stories: "Fireflies Inside a Closed Jar," "Summer Starlight"
Dust Poetry Magazine: "Ripe Oranges"
Emerge Literary Journal: "Tomorrow"
Feral: A Journal of Poetry and Art: "Our Garden at Sainte-Adresse"
Kissing Dynamite Poetry: "Disappeared Years"
Oyez Review: "Elegy"
Re-Side Magazine: "The End of Love"
Shelia-Na-Gig Online: "Joy Ride in Box Canyon," "Not a Synonym for Spanish"

Thank you also to the editors of Ghost City Press for publishing my micro-chapbook *Attachment Theory* in 2021, that includes the poem "Persimmons Burst."

Thank you to Kelli Russell Agodon, who has been a wonderful mentor to me.

Thank you to Dana Delibovi and Julie Weiss for always offering encouragement after reading my first drafts of poems.

Publisher: Leah Huete de Maines
Editor: Christen Kincaid
Cover Art: Natalie Marino
Author Photo: Joseph Rothwell
Cover Design: Elizabeth Maines McCleavy

Order online: www.finishinglinepress.com
also available on amazon.com

Author inquiries and mail orders:
Finishing Line Press
PO Box 1626
Georgetown, Kentucky 40324
USA

Table of Contents

I

Not a Synonym for Spanish 1
Elegy 2
Disappeared Years 3
Persimmons Burst 4
Tomorrow 5

II

Joy Ride in Box Canyon 9
The Bright of Old Stars 10
Ode to My Father 11
Leaving Superman 12

III

Jouissance 15
April Rain 16
Fireflies Inside a Closed Jar 17
Our Garden at Sainte-Adresse 18
Not Another Sonnet About the Moon 19
Summer Starlight 20
On the Beach 21
The End of Love 22
Constellation of Seeds 23
Ripe Oranges 24

Notes 25

I

Not a Synonym for Spanish

Mexican is watching a thousand monarchs
come home to the light of a lemon sunset,
steam from the street of a rising waterfall
when the summer rains sex in Obregón,
looking out a window at the snow
in a small mountain mining town
filled with Americans who never once tried
to roll out tortillas into flat moons,
an ode to the Aztec Talking Eagle, Cuauhtlatoatzin,
the retelling of his story when he was visited by Mary
who turned his tilma into a painting of roses,
my maternal grandmother dyeing her hair
strawberry blonde and still walking out
of a restaurant in Texas that won't serve her,
my listening in elementary school to how lazy spics are.
Mexican is my secret in adolescence,
and then breathing in the sea on the California coast
on a clear night wearing my mother's bright red shawl
just after she dies, sitting at a billowing bonfire
and following the smoke's song join her star in the sky.

Elegy

I dream I am
in your house

with its bright reds
and yellows

before the light
behind your eyes
dimmed into sea water

under dark gold sun setting
on sand,
before the tulips

wilted in the window
and released you

into the dull sky
of early evening,

before you told me
you were leaving

to become a shining star
above my garden
of new trees.

Disappeared Years

Some objects not in view—
sycamore trees hide
blue stars.

Outside the window
a donkey hovers over a foal
who knows his mother

by the shapes her hooves
make in the dirt.

Generations of women
ground corn
and stories in night bowls.

My grandmother lost her house
when she forgot
who lived there.

She can't remember
the disappeared years.

Persimmons Burst

Like light, memory changes
pink to amber.

The funeral flowers plant
themselves inside the wind's ear

while we wait
for a final forgiveness song.

Mama finally flies from the angry
tree growing in her brain.

My mouth is sewn
like a stubborn button.

A sparrow dances like a star
for the sky

and the sun bursts
into persimmons.

Tomorrow

Your plain pine box under an indigo sky
without one star and I do not know

where to go next. Had you told me
I could look for you in the trees

I would have listened to the open mouths
of leaves and their windsong stories

of tomorrow's rainbow, how even
in darkening corners of daylight

hope hides inside the scarlet sunset,
how always again the sun joins the blue water

and seagulls samba without music,
that they let love search

for color
in black and white photographs,
for gold in sand.

II

Joy Ride in Box Canyon

Before the lake disappeared,
before we knew we should wear seatbelts,
before we looked for speed limit signs,

before the fall sang out
its sour midnight whiskey
notes that we weren't the same,

before we had changed,

we sat loose and laughed
under a summer tangerine
sun, in the back of a sparkle
blue Ford pickup with its chipped
paint shining under early twilight
stars on a gravel road by bright
strawberry fields.

The Bright of Old Stars

I am lost in the opening between cypress trees
watching a blue castle of sky
open to baby birds for the first time.

I am lost listening
to the late summer bee hymns pollinating

lavender bushes, lost in memory—
of silently wanting to dance

but being too quiet to ask—
lost in remembering
my morning,

until I see the evening
and lose myself
in my own loudness

reflecting the bright
of old stars.

Ode to My Father

A summer evening
after garden hose
waterfall fights.

The afternoon
was a blue balloon,

now the sky is a field
of violets.

An early moon shines silver
and makes the grass a wild sea.

You point out
the honking geese

to the children dancing
their own joy songs
under memories of stars.

Leaving Superman

When my sister was four
she told

the neighborhood mechanic
my father had a blue suit,
a red cape.

Now my father is an old boat.
My sister and I
pretend we are superheroes

diving into dark sea water
under

constantly changing
bright star reflections.

III

Jouissance

In the dark of night
I am the sea

listening
to an orchid moon.

I turn
into a truth teller,
swimming naked

under summer stars.
I make my own joy
before the pink dawn

reading beach stones
and watching weeds

in the sand
turn into mermaids.

April Rain

Already the fields shine
with flowers.

The light of the sky

is like a blue dream
escaping
its own darkness,

but we cannot
wait here
under the sun.

Heat will tarnish
faces and force the butterflies

into hiding under the dead bark
of fallen trees.
Before the clock stops

come with me.
We can dance on the morning moon.
We can drink naked

sea water
while love lies still,

before time folds itself inside
the black permanence of yesterday,

when the world reveals
its brokenness

and stars erase themselves
into the night.

Fireflies Inside a Closed Jar

My husband's heart is a bowl
of red tulips.

Love is eating color
despite the universe.

Love is watching the open sky
with a tin telescope

while laughing at not seeing the same
bright stars.

Our Garden at Sainte-Adresse

A day at a Monet exhibit
and your hand still fits
on my shoulder.

Quiet in our seascape meditations
until I let you know what I want for our last days
even if I never learn to paint—

that we lie on a beach
like seaweed and share
the sun's last smile

on the surface
of the old waters
of the green Mediterranean
and when the evening comes

that we tell each other
stories of our beginning,

of that first night when I made you
dinner like an old wife,

of that first night when our skin
was soft as baby nectarines,

of that first night
when we laid in bed under dying stars
while falling asleep at the open window.

You ask me to listen with you
to the sad songs of the wind without wincing,

to taste unafraid
the sugar of the distant springtime
in our breaking basket of ripe plums.

Not Another Sonnet About the Moon

A walk on an empty street and my husband
asks me to hold his heart in his hand.

The sky grows dark yellow
like a field of sunflowers in the fall.

I whisper that our blood
is just as loud

as a red giant, that one day our bones
will die as bright

as a white dwarf's stardust.
We don't need to talk of definitions,

knowing at the end
we will share a sweet pear

and listen to the moon
say goodbye to the night.

Summer Starlight

A photograph taken in 1911—
my six year-old grandmother
holds hope in her eyes.

My daughters dance
the same dream.

The stems of surprise lilies
grow at night
under summer starlight

but watching time
does not stop its fall
through our fingers.

Love is catching
fireflies
in a marmalade jar.

On the Beach

Blue evening.

Seagrass sways
in a field of broken shells.

Shallow water starfish wait silently
for the wild sun setting

like a bright
orange melody at the bottom
of the sky.

We see aging stars in their high ceiling.

Shifting cloud shapes
make a marmalade of memories

while we try to remember
when we were children,

when we played
in the sand without a box.

The End of Love

Yellow is not loud.
It is the late afternoon

whispering its sweet breath
like a soft dessert
in the tiny square of a paper tray.

Yellow is a tired old sweater,
a dying leaf.

Breathtaking
in its many different shades
of grief,

yellow sounds like the hospital
discharge paper.

Someday a slow sea turtle will let go
of a dying star in October,

for yellow is the color everything
turns into.

Yellow is the end of love.

Constellation of Seeds

My body is a song
in a tree,

a constellation
of seeds in morning—

pouring itself
on the white sky—
a giant milk jug.

When I am only stardust—
after I spill

my fortunes in blue rain—
fold my body

into old stones
and give fruit
to the ocean.

Ripe Oranges

Orange blossoms explode into gold
under aging moonlight,

their sweet smell like love's fever.
The oranges are plump with spring,

and we slice them open.
Their bursting perfume

pierces the black air.
We pick them before they fall,

because we know
the stars do not see us,

because we know
we are candles

holding small flames
waiting for the wind.

NOTES

"The End of Love" was inspired by Adélia Prado's poem "Purple."

"Fireflies Inside a Closed Jar" was inspired by Melissa Studdard's poem "Because Dealthbolts Illuminate the Wonderstorm."

"Our Garden at Sainte-Adresse:" This poem refers to French impressionist painter Claude Monet's work "Garden at Sainte-Adresse."

Natalie Marino is a poet and physician. Her work appears in *Atlas and Alice*, *Gigantic Sequins*, *Isele Magazine*, *Plainsongs*, *Pleiades*, *Rust + Moth*, *The Shore*, and elsewhere. Her micro-chapbook *Attachment Theory* was published by Ghost City Press in 2021. She lives in California.

www.ingramcontent.com/pod-product-compliance
Lightning Source LLC
Chambersburg PA
CBHW022127090426
42743CB00008B/1046